Jet-pack Vet

Written by Charlotte Raby
Illustrated by Mario Gushiken

Collins

a jet pack

zig zags

a jet pack

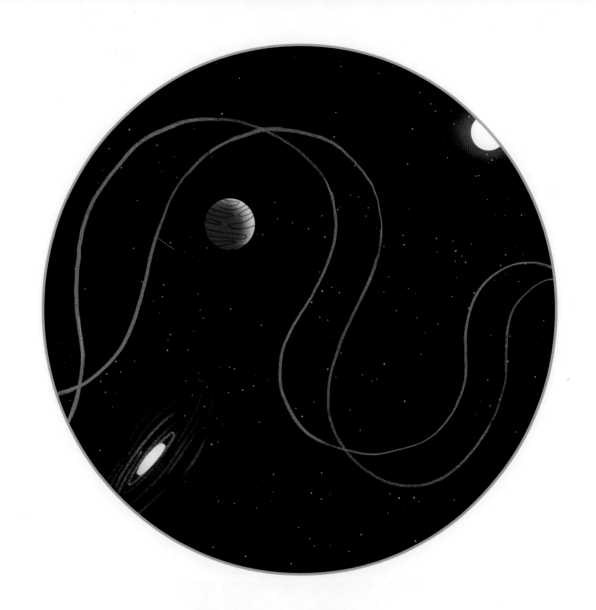

zig zags

a wet wig

the vet

a wet wig

the vet

fish and chips

red jam

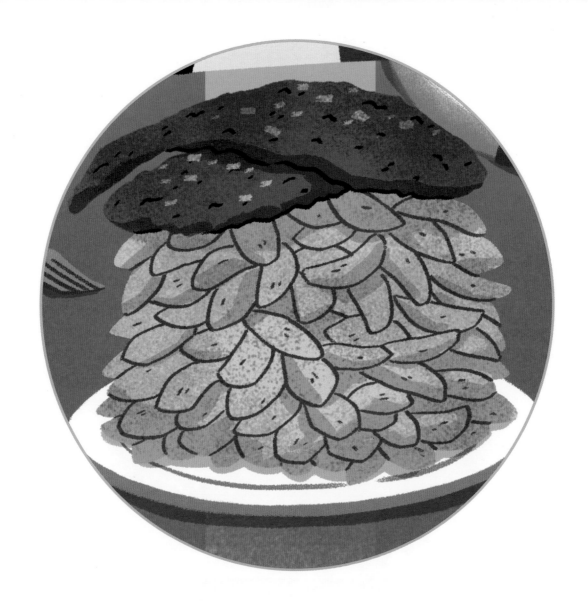

fish and chips

red jam

☙ Review: After reading ☙

Use your assessment from hearing the children read to choose any GPCs and words that need additional practice.

Read 1: Decoding

- Turn to page 3 and draw the children's attention to the 's' at the end of the word **zags**. Remind them that the 's' says /z/.
- Turn to page 10 and draw the children's attention to the 's' at the end of the word **chips**. Remind them that the 's' says /s/.
- Look at the "I spy sounds" pages (14–15) together. Ask the children to point out as many things that they can in the picture that begin with the /v/ and /j/ sounds. (*vet, violin, violets, Venus; juice, jam, jellyfish, Jupiter, jet pack*)

Read 2: Vocabulary

- Go back over the book and discuss the pictures. Encourage children to talk about details that stand out for them. Use a dialogic talk model to expand on their ideas and recast them in full sentences as naturally as possible.
- Work together to expand vocabulary by naming objects in the pictures that children do not know.
- On page 2, discuss why the pack is called a **jet pack**. Can they point to the jets in the picture?

Read 3: Comprehension

- Look together at pages 14 and 15, and discuss what the vet is doing. Ask: How might the vet be helping the animal?
- Ask children if they know anyone with a pet.